CONJURING
TRICKS

CONJURING
TRICKS

CHARLES LETTS
Letts
of London
FOUNDED 1796

This edition first published in the UK in 1992 by
CHARLES LETTS & CO LTD
Letts of London House
Parkgate Road
London SW11 4NQ

Produced by
Anness Publishing Ltd
Boundary Studios
1 Boundary Row
London SE1 8HP

ISBN: 1-85238-364-X

A CIP catalogue record for this book is available from the
British Library.

"Letts" is a registered trademark of
CHARLES LETTS & CO LTD

Editorial Director: MADAME JOANNA LORENZ
Creative Director: SIR PETER BRIDGEWATER
Text: PAUL BARNETT and RON TINER
ESQUIRES
Original Illustrations: COLONEL IVAN HISSEY
Design Magicians: SIMON BALLEY, ANNIE MOSS,
FRANCES MARR AND TERRY JEAVONS
Assisted by: JANE LANAWAY

Printed in Hong Kong

The Publishers would like to thank all those who kindly
gave permission to reproduce visual material in this book;
every effort was made to identify copyright holders and we
apologise for any inadvertent omissions.

Contents

DEDICATION

~

For ERICH WEISS *— by no means the brightest
and best of all my young students — in the wish
that, through diligent perusal of this monograph, he may add to his skills.*

A DIABOLIC WARNING

DEAR READER:

The book that you hold in your hands contains nothing that is not sweet in its innocence of intent; by deploying the Stratagems described within its pages you may entertain and amuse your friends for many hours; yet there cannot be any denial

that the showmanistic art of *conjuring* lies uncomfortably close, in the minds of some, to more DIABOLICAL arts; by which I refer, of course, to the *Occult* and *Accursed practices* of such NECROMANCERS as the young Mr. Crowley and his ilk: of which there are too many in this world of ours; and who, it is reported in the gaudier of our journals, disport themselves immodestly (even in the company of those fallen members of the *gentler sex* who are sufficiently deluded or cupiditous to partake in such designs) with the intent of inveighing the *DARK ONE HIMSELF* to influence the courses of their lives. It may seem a long distance from the naïve tricks described herein to the so-called Black Mass; but such distances are but inches to those who are sullied of heart.

Therefore, before each demonstration of your newly acquired *legerdemainiac* abilities, explain reassuringly to your audience, and especially to the children among them, that your MAGICK is but artifice, all hokus-pokus that is smiled upon by the indulgent eyes of our Good Lord, and that it smacks not one whit of the Darker Rites. And be assured in your own heart of hearts that this is the fact of the matter: while it might seem easier to use necromancy rather than artifice to pass a *thimble* through a *kerchief* – or perform such other baffling illusions as are delineated herein – in the longer term such a course may lead inexorably to the very *Damnation of your Immortal Soul*.

BE WARNED!

YOUR HUMBLE SERVANT
ARMYTAGE WARE, M.A. (OXON), D.D. (ST. ANDREWS)
1ST JANUARY 1902

THE ESSENTIALS *of* ILLUSION

*I*t is perhaps a Saturday, and afternoon tea has been taken. The children's faces are rosy with happiness but their little eyes are sleepy; the ladies are displaying that charming languor which denotes a meal of scones and cream well partaken of. None amongst the company desires that the ensuing diversions be too strenuous; yet all would wish to be entertained. It is now your moment to stride to the centre of the domestic stage, your eyes aglitter with arch wile, your pockets laden with the paraphernalia of your sleightish art. Such is the pleasing scene that might depict itself against your inner eye.

But, Reader: pause. Long ere you may impress your family and friends, first you must instruct yourself in the most *BASIC SKILLS* of the great art. Of these there are several; *viz:*— PALMING. MISDIRECTION. and, for card illusions, MAKING THE PASS. and FORCING.

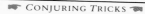

KELLAR

LEVITATION

13

PALMING

To "PALM" an object means to hold it in your hand without your audience being aware of its presence there. Most usually, the object will indeed be secreted in your palm; but this need not necessarily be the case, for sometimes it may be clasped between the fingers, as we shall see. First, however, we shall look at the ART OF PALMING in the palm itself.

Should there be an object held in your palm, it is of course essential that only the *back of your hand* should be displayed towards your audience. This is a habit which it is easier to describe than it is to accustom yourself to;

for as we speak naturally to our fellows we tend to move our hands freely; and in front of your audience you must continue to dissemble such randomness of motion while yet ensuring that it never becomes obvious to them that you are permitting them to see only your hand's back. In short,

you must perform the *Unnatural* while making it seem wholly *Natural*. The best way to attain this end is to practise before a mirror. With or without an object in one palm, *hold a discourse with your reflection,* moving your hands in such a wise as seems spontaneous, yet being cautious that only the rear of the hand concerned is ever in view. At first your movements will be clumsy and strained, so that you may recall one of *Mr. Stanislavski's puppers;* yet as you continue to prate at your reflection you will find, after some exercise, that the trick is within your ability.

One point in particular to note: at no time, when in the presence of an audience, should you turn your own gaze (even, or especially, in a furtive manner, to see that all is well) towards the hand that conceals; for to do so is to invite your spectators to do likewise; so that then they will observe

that one side of your hand is forever hidden from them. Instead, be ostentatious with your other hand, casting it about with **FLAMBOYANCE**, so that the natural inclination of your audience's eyes will be to follow ☞

it; and thereby the very presence of your other hand will go ignored.

Imagine that the object you wish to palm is a card. Hold your hand in front of you, palm upwards, and see how the fingers naturally curve upwards a little. If you then place the card on your hand such that its upper edge rests along the grooves of your first inner knuckles, you will find that you can make minor adjustment to the curvature of your fingers such that the lower edge of the card lodges itself against the ball of your thumb and the bulge of your hand's base. (If your hands are small, you may find it easier, for all the tricks described in this monograph, to use the **DWARF-SIZED CARDS** that are sometimes sold for use in games of Patience.) The card thus securely held, your hand, viewed from its back, will seem to be poised quite naturally; although the careful observer will soon notice the stillness of its pose and suspect your *Subterfuge*. As we saw, it is your chore to ensure that none choose to observe carefully; you may elect to keep your hand by your side.

A larger coin, like a half-crown or especially a crown, may be retained ☛

in the centre of the palm itself. Should you slightly cup your hand, in addition to bringing the ball of your
thumb towards the palm's centre, the coin can be securely clutched while, once again, betraying nothing of its

presence to those who see only your
hand's back. Smaller coins may be
lodged between the grooves at the
base of your third inner knuckles and
those at the base of the second or first
inner knuckles.

A further technique for use with coins, often called
PALMING although it does not involve the
palm, is to hold the coin tightly between
the bases or stems of two adjacent fingers,
such that the coin protrudes from one
side of the hand only, at either front or
rear; the thin rim of the coin will not be
visible between the fingers' flesh when viewed from the
converse side of the hand. The great advantage of this
method is that it enables you, should the disc of the coin
be protruding from the rear of the fingers, to display

your open palm for all to see that
it is empty; as if, perhaps, you
were pronouncing the *benediction*
at the conclusion of the offering,
although of course you must not

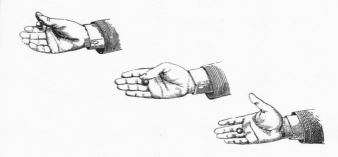

spread your fingers, as else the coin will drop. A small card (as described above) may be similarly held.

Practice is important in all the divisions of *LEGER-DEMAIN*, but nowhere more so than in the basic art of palming. Satisfy yourself before your mirror that you have it to a "Tee", perhaps an hour each evening in the privacy of the bedchamber before you retire; but ensure that none of your family detect your habit, for, should they do so, then all of your other *Subterfuges* will be as naught, for your audience will believe all to have been accomplished through palming, and will cease to marvel.

MISDIRECTION

WE NOTED in the context of palming that you should never cast a glance at the hand in which an object is secreted, but instead focus your attention on something else, perhaps your other hand; for in so doing you focus your audience's attention, also, upon that innocent object. This is the skill known as "MIS-DIRECTION"; for through its use you are diverting the gaze of your audience towards what is, for the SCEPTICS among them, the *wrong direction*.

Bear in mind ever that adroitness of your fingers and hands (and later, perhaps of your nether limbs) is not in itself sufficient; you must augment your dexterity with Stratagems designed to turn the attention of your audience elsewhere, so that you may achieve your aim covertly. This can often be done through an *exaggeration* of all those movements which are in themselves irrelevant to your ends; most especially those movements which you seek to persuade your onlookers

are important when in fact they are not. Imagine that you wish to make a coin appear in your right hand. All the secret parts of the trick will be performed by your left; but to your

audience it must seem as if the *"MAGICK"* is centred on your right; so you must display the right with a great show of significance, and *concentrate your gaze upon it yourself* as you flex its fingers through the air and rotate it to show its prior emptiness. All the movements of your body will be speaking to the spectators, and telling them that your right hand is the focus of the action; they will concentrate, as you are doing, upon that hand, anticipating that, through close observation of it, they will be able to expose your *Artifice*; yet all the while your left hand is about its covert business, disregarded.

The disposition of your body is, then, your most important tool of *Misdirection*. Yet it may be substantially augmented by the words you speak the while; this monologue is dubbed, among those skilled in the conjuring arts, "patter". Although, before the start of your performance, you should have reassured your willing captives that no *Satanism* is involved in your craft (as we

saw), lest the ladies and children later suffer nightmares; during the performance proper you should maintain the pretence that **Magick** is indeed involved. Keep talking at all times during the early stages of your trick – perhaps to say that, while you have no faith in **Magick** yourself, yet an OLD ORIENTAL GENTLEMAN once showed you this trick-which-is-not-a-trick, for try as you might, you, like others, can find no sleight of hand in it, yet always *its result is the impossible!* Then, if you are astonished by the **"Magick"** as you accomplish your effect, the audience will be likewise filled with amaze. Or you may elect some quite different *line* (as it is called) of "patter"; here there is scope for your imagination, such as it may be. You might even dissemble that you are honestly explaining to the company all the workings of the sleight, so that they may try it for themselves afterward; then watch with mirth their own futile, frustrated attempts, and slowness to recognize the *jest*.

FORCING

*W*hether or not one will later MAKE THE
PASS, *many card-tricks depend upon the
illusionist's ability first of all to "force" the
UNWITTING SPECTATOR to select a card that
has earlier been determined upon by the
illusionist himself. There are various modes
of executing this manoeuvre, of which here
are two.*

Fan the cards out, as if in a random manner, but surreptitiously, with the thumb of the retaining hand, push forward the card of your choice so that its tip protrudes just a very little (cave that it is not too far) beyond those of the others; the SPECTATOR must not be aware of the protrusion. You should be aware of which members of your audience are least likely to have their wits about them; go to one of these, and request that this person be the one to assist you in your illusion by taking a card from the fan. In most instances, the slight PROTRUSION of the chosen card will be enough to persuade her dainty hand to fall upon it; should her fingers PERVERSELY stray toward a different region of the fan, it is no difficult matter, with feigned casualness, slightly to alter the position of your hands such as to rotate the fan a little, until the chosen card is beneath her hand. If all else fails, break off in mid-"patter", as if you had suddenly remembered an Important Item of which you had earlier forgot to apprise the audience; and then resume as before, perhaps this time with a fittingly more GULLIBLE MEMBER of their number.

A quite different mode of procedure is, first, to insure that the card you wish to be selected is at the bottom of the deck. Then ask the subject to CUT THE DECK RANDOMLY. Place the upper pile, face downward, on his hand and, talking rapidly the while, promptly place the other half of the deck crosswise on top of the first. Now ask him to look at the bottom card of the second pile. Of course, this is the card that you had earlier placed at the base of the deck as a whole; but the ILLUSION is very convincing that it is, rather, the card to which the subject randomly cut, at your behest. It is the very simplicity of the manoeuvre that causes this misconception on the subject's part!

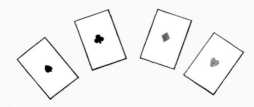

I have disserted at length upon these tech-
niques, because of their most essential
nature. They are your four *basic tools:*
armed with them, you may break open the
door to a room brim-full of Illusion; whereas without them, you are as nothing.

MAKING *the* PASS

The object of MAKING THE PASS is to bring a particular card to the topmost position in a deck. This basic move requires skill and, as in all conjuring, much practice before you can perform it to perfection; yet, once that degree of facility has been attained, *COUNTLESS CARD TRICKS* lie within your grasp. There are two ways in which it may be accomplished: the better; and the easier. Are not matters always thus?

You have fanned out the cards and required one of the onlookers to SELECT A CARD; now he is to return it. He sees you offering the deck to him in a single pile; he slips his card in among the rest, and seemingly indistinguishable from them; yet a little later, after whatever other **Hokuspokus** is entailed in the illusion, his card MAGICKALLY reappears.

The *better* way of achieving this effect follows:— As the card is pushed back into the deck, use the fingers of your left hand, clasping the edges of the cards, to slightly buckle them such that they form discrete upper and lower piles, with the inserted card then lying atop the lower pile. The fingers of your left hand should be wrapped around the deck as a whole; move the outer two fingers so that their nails enhance the division between the two piles; while these two lock the lower packet in position, the other two fingers may, by friction, draw the upper pile off towards one side. With your right hand, *act swiftly* as if merely to tidy the single deck; but instead, with the fingertips, push the lower deck into the crease of the ball of your left hand's thumb; flexion of the thumb as a whole will then tilt the lower deck upward, angling it against the edges of the cards in the upper deck. Your right hand still momentarily concealing what happens, the fingers of your left hand can speedily manipulate the lower pile beneath the upper; and now the card your acquaintance selected is on top of the deck as a whole.

This exercise may appear *dauntingly difficult*; and, indeed, I found it a trifle hard myself at first; yet with sufficient practice you will find that you can perform it almost reflexively, such that the manipulation is invisible to even the most kestrel-eyed of observers; perhaps a couple hours of practice of an evening for a month or more will be an adequacy of rehearsal

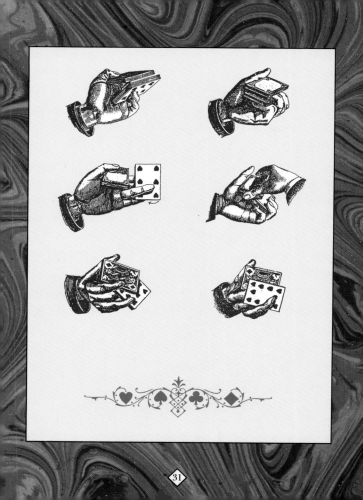

for certain ladies or simpletons; a man with all his wits may need a week.

The *easier* method is to insert the little finger of your left hand in at the place where the card is returned. Now you may riffle the ends of the deck, as if to show that it preserves its integrity; yet do not overtly direct your attention, or your audience's, towards it. Clamp your vision with that of the person who has returned the card, so that he must needs break your gaze in order to glance down at your hands; this, if he has COURTESY, he will be unwilling to do. Now, as if it is a matter of no import, cut the cards, seemingly at random, but in fact at the place your little finger is marking; and proceed ostentatiously to *RIFFLE-SHUFFLE* the pack; in which exercise it is a simple enough matter to insure that the chosen card remains always at the deck's head. (Such shuffling should also succeed employment of the *better* method described above.)

CIRCUS BUSC

Die Sensation:
Der unersättliche
MAC NORTO
Das menschliche
Aquarium ::::::::

SPELLING
the CARD

Explain to the audience that a pedagogic acquaintance of yours is of such ability that he has succeeded in teaching even packs of cards the three "Rs", as they are called; in especial, he has instructed the very deck you have in your hand in the rudiments of spelling. Ask a member of the audience to select a card; and then you must MAKE THE PASS such that the card is at the top of the deck. Ask the subject to tell you the card's name; and proceed to spell it out as you deal the cards out, face-down, letter by letter as you spell. Imagine the card is the *Knave (or Jack) of Diamonds*; then say "K", as you lay out the first card, "N", for the second, and so forth until at length you reach the "S" of *Diamonds*.

Turn up this last card and show it. Oh! – the mortification you affect! It is not at all the card you expected! Muttering an audible reproof to yourself, explain you forgot aforehand to utter the MAGICKAL INCANTATION – "*Ongaeins*", or "*Munsie*", or "*Fupperty-jig*", or some such nonce-word as skips to your lips – and do so now as you drop this last of the cards atop the face-down heap you have dealt out. Pick up the heap (at the bottom of which, you know but the audience does not, is the Knave of Diamonds) and put it with the rest of the deck. Cry out your INCANTATION, and then ask the subject himself to spell out "his" card, as before. This time, of course, the last card he deals proves to be the one he chose!

DISAPPEARANCE OF A SILVER DOLLAR.

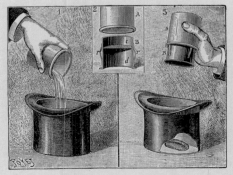

FIGS. 1-3.—A CAKE BAKED IN A HAT.

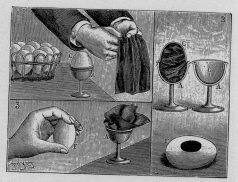

TRICK WITH AN EGG AND HANDKERCHIEF.

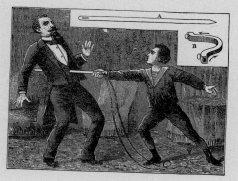

A SWORD TRICK.

THE VAIN CARD

HERE AGAIN is a trick that depends on your ability to *MAKE THE PASS*. Tell your **agog spectators** that cards, like people, have *personalities;* and that they can be as guilty of the Seven Sins as might any mortal be, most notably the sin of VANITY. This statement may give rise to a little scepticism among the gentlemen present; take this as your cue to demonstrate the veracity of your claim.

Have a subject select a card; then MAKE THE PASS to bring it to the head of the deck, as always. While continuing to pronounce upon the *Vaingloriousness* of cards – as great as any woman's – divert the audience with your wit and drollery long enough that their acuity is allayed. Then in one hand hold up the deck, the face of the lowermost card being towards your audience. Gripping the edges of the deck firmly with your thumb and two outer fingers, quite naturally, use your middle two fingers to "walk" against the rear of the hindmost card; so that it slowly rises, seemingly from the middle of the deck, to show its face above its fellows.

Be modest in response to the *applause*; it would not do to trip into the same *moral pitfall* as did the card!

8

THE INFORMATIVE
CARD

This is an illusion that requires little or no dexterity, yet its simplicity is such that it may delude even the most sophisticated of audiences. It is wise to use it as the first trick of your performance, as otherwise its lack of ostentation may pall alongside some of the other effects you can achieve. Shuffle the deck, and unobtrusively note the BOTTOM-MOST *card. Request of one of the company that he pick a card, in the usual fashion; and while he is looking at it (but not informing you of its value), cut the pack at random and put the two packets on your table. Take the card from him and idly toss it on top of one of the packets, which is in*

fact the PACKET *that was* UPPERMOST *when the deck was entire! Or, you may ask the subject to place* "his" card there himself. Either way, now place the other packet on top of this one, such that the chosen card is seemingly lost amid its fellows. You may now, with caution, lightly shuffle the deck (although you must make it seem as if your shuffling is a rigorous one). Now deal out the cards from the top of the deck, turning them up as you do so. Mutter much HOKUS-POKUS; more loudly, apprise your audience that your Magickal instincts are telling you that you are approaching, closely and yet more closely, the card you seek. BUILD UP EXCITEDLY; then, as you turn up the card that was once the bottom-most — great elation! — **your Magickal faculties are singing!** — the

chosen card is so close now that it must be — it MUST be! — the very next! And, as you turn it up, so of course it is.

BALANCING
a COIN *on*
a BLADE

*T*his is a trick that can be done cosily, at the Dinner-table, or grandly, as the climax to one of your more flamboyant displays; in the former instance, you will use an ordinary *TABLE-KNIFE*; in the latter, should you have one, a *SWORD*, perhaps a trophy from your time in the **Colonies**. Ask among the company for the loan of a florin or half-crown; when one is forth-coming, accept it profusely. Unbeknownst to the **spectators**, you have already to hand an-other florin or half-crown which you have *prepared in advance* by coating one side of it with shoemaker's or even plain candle wax. As you receive the lent coin, make a pal-aver about fetching the blade – reaching

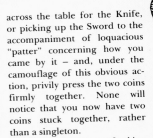

across the table for the Knife, or picking up the Sword to the accompaniment of loquacious "patter" concerning how you came by it – and, under the camouflage of this obvious action, privily press the two coins firmly together. None will notice that you now have two coins stuck together, rather than a singleton.

With a great show of taking care, and remarks as to the infinite degree of bodily stillness you require to perform this feat, hold the blade horizontally, sharp edge uppermost; and set the doubleton coin upright on it, such that the blade fits into the groove between the two coins. Now, with a mighty wave of your free hand, you can show the *spectators* that you

have succeeded in your aim; and sometimes, if you are fortunate, you may even be able, by inclining the blade appropriately, to make the doubleton run BACKWARDS AND FORWARDS along it; but this is not a good fortune that you can with **Confidence** predict (so much depends on how the coins have adhered), so mention nothing of it until the time for experiment has come.

After removing the doubleton from its perch, separate its two components unobtrusively with the nail of your thumb; and hand the original coin back to its owner, disposing of the waxed coin covertly.

THE CALLING
of the CARDS

*H*ere is a more complicated illusion than most, and it requires you to perform a deal of preparation aforehand; also, you must purchase two identical packs of cards in order to achieve your aim (those sold by Messrs. Smith at 9d. per pack are quite adequate).

The effect is this:– You pass a pack of cards to your audience and instruct them to shuffle as they will, passing the pack among themselves until all are well scrambled. You retrieve the pack and, by dint of loudly cried **hokus-pokus,** are able to name each of the cards in the entire pack as it is turned up by a member of the gathering.

Before the start, you have opened the reserve pack of cards and have arranged them in an order which seems to be RANDOM but which is in fact easy to recall. For example, the suits are, in alphabetical order: *Clubs, Diamonds, Hearts,* and *Spades;* and the cards themselves, similarly deployed, are: *Ace, Deuce, Eight, Five, Four, King, Knave (Jack), Nine, Queen, Seven, Six, Ten, Trey.* Thus a seeming disorder may be created by following both alphabets together, *viz:*– ACE OF CLUBS, DEUCE OF DIAMONDS, EIGHT OF HEARTS, FIVE OF SPADES ... until at last the *Trey of Spades* is reached.

The *RESERVE PACK*, so arranged, is concealed privily about your person prior to the commencement. Once the decoy pack has been shuffled and returned to you, it is easy enough – perhaps on the pretext that you have left your **Magickal Wand** (or suchlike Tomfoolery) on the table behind you – to turn your back on your audience briefly, for just long enough that you may execute the substitution of the two packs. Then, Wand waved and Psychic Spells incanted, you proceed to dazzle your audience with your TELEPATHIC POWERS.

Even should they guess that there is some trickery involved, even that there has been a substitution, they will still marvel at your feat of memory, in recalling *FIFTY-TWO* cards in an obviously random arrangement!

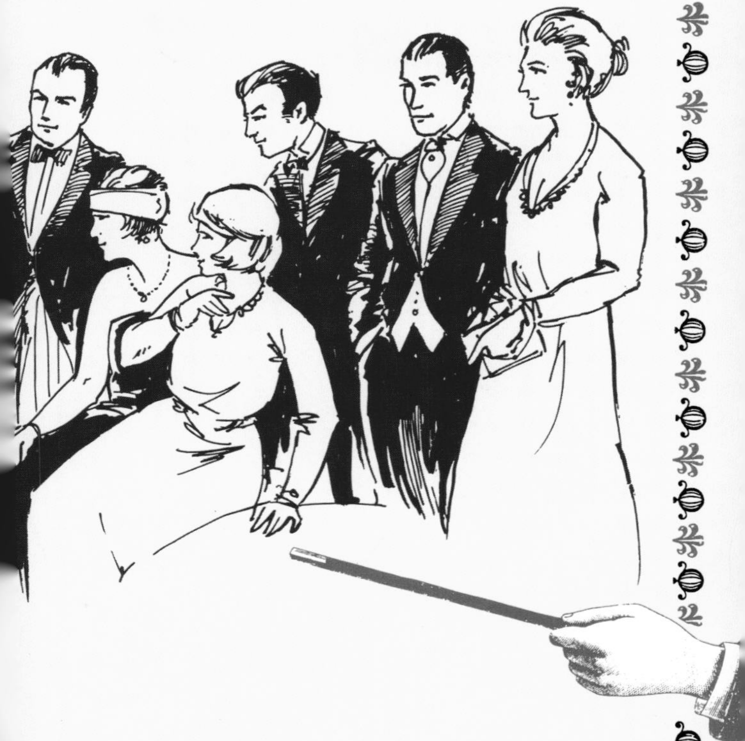

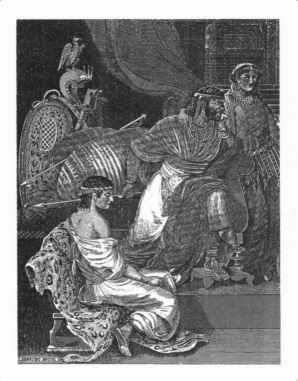

A LATIN CHARM

I F THE PAGAN TYRANT Js. Caesar is to be believed, it was in the year 51 before Our Lord that one among his generals, a certain *Mutus Andronius Burrus,* gave their name to an equally pagan people of Western Gaul, calling them the *COCI;* hence the schoolboy tag: *Mutus nomen Coci dedit;* from the *De Bello Gallico,* iii, 16. It may indeed be that the forthcoming trick was devised around the time that the militarist was penning his memoirs; certes Erich Weiss believes it to have been so, for it is upon this pretty phrase that the illusion depends.

In the days preceding your presentation, memorize the phrase: practise saying it silently to yourself until you are assured that, even in the excitement of the performance, it will come naturally to the forefront of your mind. Once about to perform the trick, tell your audience that it is a feat of Magick brought down to us from the ANCIENT EGYPTIANS, or the HINDOOS, or the MAYA: but do not mention the **ROMANS,** for that might put the thought of Caesar's remark in some gentleman's mind. *Now shuffle your deck,* and deal out the first twenty cards from it, arranging them into ten pairs. Call for a volunteer; and, as he comes forth, ask him to choose, in his mind alone, one of the pairs, and to remember the two cards concerned.

That done, gather together the cards, but keep them in their pairs. Now is the time you will be glad you went to such pains to memorise the tag! You will be dealing out the cards again, face-upward, and seemingly in a completely unpreconceived order. In fact, however, the order will have been carefully determined, for you have imagined that Caesar's words are set out on your table as follows ☞

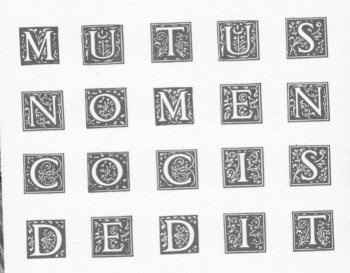

As you lay out the cards, do so as follows. The first card goes in the position of the "M" in the first row; the second card goes in the third position of the second row, again according to the "M". For the next card (the third), set it in the position of the first "U", and with the card succeeding, the other "U"; and so forth until all the cards are laid. Now you must ask the subject to tell you in which row or rows the two cards of his selected coupling appear; from this information it will, clearly, be a CHILD-PLAY for you to determine the cards concerned; as will be evident to you now from study of the array shown.

The feat is most impressive should you ask several members of the company to select Pairs all at the same time; for then, on being appraised by each of the rows in which their selections appear, you can reel off the identities of the twinned cards with awe-inspiring speed, each after the next.

★ ★ ★ ★ ★ ★ ★

THE FOUR SCURVY KNAVES

~

There is a very well known trick whereby the four Knaves (or Jacks), donning the mantle of thieves (for the purpose of the Trick), are seemingly made to foregather at the top of the house – that is, the deck – despite having been placed in different positions within the house. The effect is achieved by palming three extra cards. On drawing the KNAVES from the deck at the start of the trick, you place them over the three

EARLIER-PURLOINED cards, such that it appears as if the only cards in your hand are the four Knaves. Telling a story of four thieves robbing a house, you deal

off one card at a time from the BACK of this small traitorous pile, declaring as you go that each of them is a Knave. The first thief went to the basement (a card to the bottom of the deck), the next to the ground floor (a card to the lower part of the deck), the next to the  first floor (a card to the upper part of the deck), and the fourth to the roof (placing seemingly one card, but in fact all four knaves, on the top of the deck). Then the **Police** approach (a Magickal Wand is waved, or something similar), and the thieves all rush to the roof of the house (you deal off the four KNAVES from the top of the deck).

These days, however, this last effect is rarely greeted with the desiredly fervent gasp of awe-strickenness and wonderment; for the trick is now known to even the most pol-troonish of children and servants, and is a great favourite among them.

But the trick I now out-line profits from the very fact that it is NOT effec-ted in the wise described above; thus your audience watches hawkishly for ☛

what they anticipate you to do, whereas the very simple actions you are in fact performing go unnoticed.

Start by pulling the KNAVES from wherever they are sequestered within the deck: even better, desire that one of the assemblage does this for you. Begin your story as before. There are four Thieves, &c., &c., and the first of them goes to the basement of the house; here you baffle sceptics, for you **quite brazenly** display the face of the card as you place it in its allotted site. This initial incredulity transmutes to something greater as you do likewise with the next card, announcing that the second thief went straight to the roof (notice the alteration of the tale's order). Now you cut the pack, as if absently, the while looking at the remaining two "THIEVES", which you have arranged to be of the same col-

our (that is, Hearts with Diamonds, or Clubs with Spades). You break off to explain that the third and fourth thieves were brothers, as can be told from their shared colours; and that they were but timorous burglars, as can be deduced from their unwillingness to go to either of the

vulnerable extremities (roof or basement) of the house. With a little skill, you can devise your PATTER such that your audience breaks into laughter, describing, as you do, pathetically, the quaking plight of the two cowardly brothers!

Whatever, you have distracted the onlookers long enough that – as you conclude with the remark that the two brothers, unwilling to be out of each other's sight, went together to the

WHERE'S THE BURGLAR?

middle of the house – long enough, as I say, so that your audience notices nothing amiss as you place the final two KNAVES on top of one of the piles – then place the other pile atop them; thereby seemingly consigning those cards to the deck's centre. But in fact this is not so: for you have placed them on what was the UPPER packet of the deck; and have placed what was the LOWER packet over them. Thus, unperceived by your spectators, you have brought all four "thieves" together in the centre of the "house".

Now employ your "patter" once more. **THRILL** your audience with the rush of the PEELERS to the place; evoke the terrors of the thieves as they hear the advance of The Law; describe how the thieves gather, not knowing where to run, on the middle storey of the house; and there – aha! – they are apprehended by CHIEF SUPERINTENDENT MAGICKO and his stalwarts . . . as you display with a FLOURISH by spreading out the cards face-up!

CATCH *a* FALLING CARD

Here is an illusion that was taught to me many years ago, and which is a *Sleight* of no little elegance. It requires a tiny preparation beforehand; to wit, the placing of a dab of honey at the rear edge of your table.

In the usual way, ask some member of the company to select a card; now you must MAKE THE PASS to bring their card to the head of the pack. Place the pack on the table, and cut it. Explain to all that it is a little-known fact that cards are possessed of *INVISIBLE WINGS*, such that they can fly, but only a very little, just enough that, if thrown, they can to some extent determine their landing-place. Explain also that you have already used your **PSYCHIC POWERS** to infer the selected card, and that, even though you as yet know not its location within the deck, you will call it to you such that it lands, falconlike, on your hand.

With one hand, pick up
the pack of cards in which
the "key" card is *not;* simul-
taneously, touch the back of
your other hand to the concealed blob of honey, so that
your skin becomes sticky. Make a great show of throw-
ing the first pack of cards vertically upward into the
air, so that they flutter down about you; and in the
commotion, swiftly use the sticky back of your other
hand to touch and pick up the "key" card (which as you
will recall is on top of the other pack). No one will
notice your hand making this detour as you move it out
to the centre of the descending shower, and it will seem
as if one card did indeed elect to swoop down to make
its Perch on the back of your *Outstretched Hand.*

Timing is of the essence in this illusion, so practise
it well beforehand. Also, because of the *stickiness* both
on your hand and, now, on the back of the
"key" card, it is as well that this be the
CONCLUDING TRICK of your performance.

THE MAGICIAN ANNUAL

Compiled & Edited By
WILL GOLDSTON

The
MAGICIAN ANNUAL
1910—11.

The Publishers beg to announce that owing to the enormous demand for this book, intending purchasers should order early to avoid disappointment. There will be no reprint.

4/6 POST FREE
4/10

Copies may be obtained of all Magical Dealers and Booksellers, or direct of

A. W. GAMAGE, Ltd., Holborn, London, E.C.

100 PAGES ART PAPER — **EARLY IN NOVEMBER** — FOUR COLOR PLATES

ARTISTIC COVER HANDSOMELY BOUND IN CLOTH

THE WONDERSOME TUMBLER

*A*lthough this trick is most baffling when performed on your illusionist's table as part of a **Recital of Mystery,** it may just as easily be done on the DINING-TABLE in the wake of a repast, when the impact of its illusion may be doubled. All that you require by way of equipment are (*openly*) a Tumbler part-filled with water and (*covertly*) a spent Match-stick, which perhaps you may obtain

from the gardener. The latter (that is, the match-stick) you secrete beneath the tablecloth in advance.

Taking the tumbler of water, you explain that you are about to perform a nigh-**miraculously** difficult feat of *BALANCING*. Your audience sees you tilt the tumbler at an angle, and attempt to steady it in that position. Of course, the achievement is difficult even for you, you explain, as the tumbler wobbles about on your first ☞

couple of essays; but then, the third time (when, unbeknownst to your onlookers, you have located the "*bump*" of the matchstick beneath the cloth), you draw your hands away cautiously and – *WONDER OF WONDERS!* – the tumbler stays poised, seemingly in a perfectly arranged balance! (This is in truth quite reasonably difficult to effect, even with the matchstick present; so it is wise to *practise! practise! practise!* as always.) Now you catch the tumbler swiftly, as if it were about to fall, and pass it to someone near to you, suggesting that they attempt to emulate your feat.

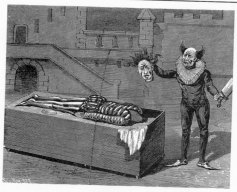

A THIMBLE THROUGH *a* KERCHIEF

HERE YOU SEEM to pass a thimble part-way through a handkerchief. Most bracing of all, it is a borrowed handkerchief, preferably that of a **lady**, who will squeal with distracting dismay as she sees, as she thinks, her dainty silken scrap destroyed; before it is returned whole to her, and she is reassured that all is well.

You need, in truth, two thimbles; and must prevail upon the gardener or his boy to effect some advance preparation for you. The two thimbles should be of thin, smooth metal, such as the tawdry ones that can be picked up for ha'pence at any market-stall; and one must be slightly larger than the other, such that it will fit loosely over it. Have your labourer place the larger one over the end of a suitably-sized piece of dowel-rod; cut it with a hack-saw or such other implement as he deems fit, until only the upper part of the thimble remains. The detrital ring of its lower segment is discarded, and then the edge of the tip smoothed with a fine-grained file. At last the tip should be such that it may be *fitted over* the smaller thimble such that its presence is not obvious save under the closest scrutiny. 🍂

At trick's start the Thimble (with its "hat") is on your table. You call for the loan of a kerchief before explaining what it is you intend to do; for obvious reasons, do not accept any kerchief proffered by a child, especially a boy. Whilst waiting for the kerchief, pick up your treated thimble with your left hand, and fit it over the end of your index finger; in so doing, it is no tricky matter to palm the prepared thimble-tip. Take the hankie in your left hand; hold your right index finger vertically upwards; and drape the cloth over it loosely, prattling as you do so of your intentions. Inform the **aghast lady** that her kerchief shall not suffer; yet seem doubtful as you do so, as if

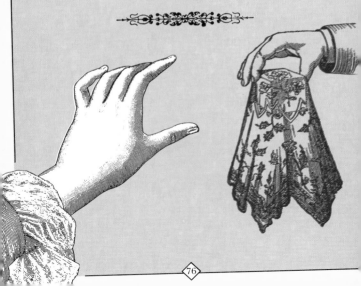

you yourself are uncertain. *Smooth down the cloth* with regular, slow strokings of your left hand as you go, smiling reassuringly at the kerchief's owner; and, on one of your passes, ADROITLY slip the thimble-tip into position, firming it in place with a little extra pressure of your fingers or thumb.

To all and sundry, it will seem as if you have indeed penetrated the thimble through the cloth. As ABIGAIL runs to fetch the salts, continue to stroke as before, and this time on one of your passes, re-palm the thimble-tip. Remove the kerchief to the onset of the *Applause*; and in the act of tugging the thimble from off of your finger, replace its "hat", so that then you are able to show your hands untenanted, save by the (seemingly!) SINGLE THIMBLE with which you commenced.

THE MAGNETIC SALT CELLAR

This marvellously impressing trick is best performed at a meal's end. Explain to your fellow-diners that you have recently been re-reading PROF. MESMER's classic studies on MAGNET-ISM, and that before the meal you have taken the precaution of rubbing your body with an ELECTRO-MAGNET, thus charging yourself with magnetic flux, so that now you are able to weakly attract metallic objects towards you. As the company guffaws at your claims, cast your eye about for some **metallic object** — and lo!: your gaze fastens on the metal top of the Salt Cellar. With your hand pointing downwards, its back to the onlookers, you touch your very finger-tips to the salt-cellar's perforated top:

slowly **raise your hand**, and the salt-cellar miraculously follows!

All that you have done is, just before making your preliminary boast, to lodge a WOODEN TOOTH-PICK between your ring-finger and its ring, the pick running along the length of your finger, its point at about the same level as the end of your finger-nail. As you put your fingers on the cellar's top, it is easy to curl them a trifle, and to jab the end of the tooth-pick into one of the holes in the cellar's top. After all have marvelled, it is a matter of simplicity, on replacing the cellar on the table, to straighten your fingers a little, so as to force the cellar off the wooden point.

MASTER COLUMBUS'S OTHER TECHNIQUE

here is a famous tale that Columbus, on his return from his trans-oceanic cruise, was asked by the courtiers assembled at the festive board how it was he had known beforehand that the World was round. In particular, the scoffers suggested that *anyone else* could have executed the vaunted voyage as well as he. To this the grizzled navigator retorted: *"But can anyone here balance an egg on its end?"* After they had all said nay, or attempted the exploit unsuccessfully, he took an egg from its dish, crushed its end with a blow on the table; and then stood the egg, as desired. When his detractors shouted that this was a simple, puerile, trick, he stared upon them with a rimey, gimlet eye, and said: "Yes – *when you know how.*"

Tell your audience this story, as if they had not heard it a thousand times before; then add that this was not at all what Columbus did. Before their astonished countenances, you proceed to take a plain white egg (borrowed for the purpose, perhaps, from Cook), which you allow them to examine to verify its plain-ness and

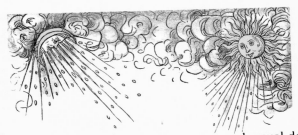

whiteness, and then with an easy grace and casual demeanour, balance the egg on its end! After, you give back the egg again; and still it is obviously nothing more nor less than an egg.

The trick is that you have a WHITE CLOTH draping your table – as well you might in any event – and beforehand you made a trifling mound of salt on the cloth; white against white, the salt will be invisible. It is on this mound that you place the egg, which will make there a temporary Cuplet for itself. As the rest examine the egg, between applauses, it is easy for you, with a nonchalant sweep of the hand, to brush away the evidence of your **innocent deception.**

THE NAMING of CARDS

"**M**agick", you must announce to the assembly, "does not isolate itself to MAGICIANS solely, for it is within the power of all of us to perform feats of wizardry, as I will shortly demonstrate". (This statement is not in fact true, be it noted; but you should proclaim it with conviction.) Then take your pack of cards and have it shuffled by one or more among the company, until all are content that it is a thorough mish-mash. Now spread out all the cards, *willy-nilly*, upon the surface of your table; surreptitiously noting the while the position of one of them: perhaps the card that was at the base of the shuffled deck. Tell the audience that, under your tutelage, their ☞

innate *MYSTICAL POWERS* will enable them to pick out from the spread, the *precise* cards that you dictate.

Imagine the card whose position you know is the ACE, or ONE, OF SPADES. Tell the first subject that he must use his discretion to select the ACE OF SPADES from those arranged, face-down, in front of him, and to tap its back. At long last, his mind made up, he does so. You pick up the card,

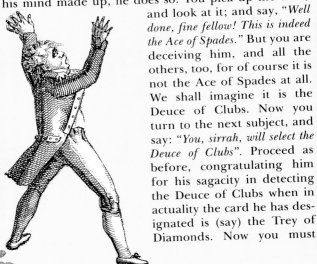

and look at it; and say, *"Well done, fine fellow! This is indeed the Ace of Spades."* But you are deceiving him, and all the others, too, for of course it is not the Ace of Spades at all. We shall imagine it is the Deuce of Clubs. Now you turn to the next subject, and say: *"You, sirrah, will select the Deuce of Clubs"*. Proceed as before, congratulating him for his sagacity in detecting the Deuce of Clubs when in actuality the card he has designated is (say) the Trey of Diamonds. Now you must

ask the next person to pick
out the Trey of Diamonds;
and so you continue for at
most five or six times:
then, with the last card that
has been chosen (say, the
Ten of Hearts), cry: *"And
at last it is time for my own
essay. I shall endeavour to
find the Ten of Hearts."* So
saying, you pick up the
Ace of Spades and join it
with the others you have
collected in your hand.

Imagine the delightful consternation of the assembly
when you fan out the cards to show that they have
indeed, unknowing, heard the *ASTRAL COUNSELLORS*
guiding their choice!

Once small chance may make this feat yet more
mysterious. A subject may pick up the Ace of Spades.
In which case, there is an end on't; for the members of
the audience have (it seems), without any intervention
on your part, selected the requisite Cards.

A **10/–** Trick

Y OU ARE standing in front of an audience, and ask for a *10/– note* or *dollar bill* (if your company is affluent, perhaps you might even request £1 0s 0d; but then this trick involves your having an equivalent note of your own; and this is a large sum for, say, those on a stipend). Request that its owner crumple it into a ball and toss it to you; the ball caught, hold it in your two hands, as if concentrating on it; then toss it to someone else, asking him to open it out. Furrowing your brow in intense **Telepathic Thought,** you slowly enunciate the SERIAL NUMBER on the note!

Clearly you could not have had time to MEMORIZE the number; besides, with the note crumpled, the number was never open to your view. What you have done, of course, is to have about you a different *crumpled-up note*, its serial number *already learnt*. This you have *PALMED* in your left hand immediately prior to trick's start; catching the thrown note with your right, you have exchanged it for your own, palming it in its turn; so that the note tossed to the other **subject** is one whose number you already know. The OWNER of the original, on its return, will never notice that the substitution has occurred.

THE *BALANCING MAGICKAL WAND*

Imagine that, as part of your repertory, you are standing making idle conversation with the audience (it is not idle conversation, of course, but carefully rehearsed "patter"); when the MAGICKAL WAND in your hand, seemingly unnoticed by you, suddenly appears to take on an independent life; balancing itself in all sorts of impossible poses. When the **gasps** of the audience draw your attention to your "prop's" behaviour, you **rebuke** it, strike it a gentle blow; and then, on the request that is sure to come, pass it around for the audience to inspect at will, to prove to themselves that it has not been "RIGGED".

The secret is that, beforehand, you have possessed yourself of a long strand from the head of a FAIR-HAIRED lady; my own good wife has copious silvery hair which, pluck'd as she sleeps, serves excellently; but you can make your own arrangements. This Strand you tie to form a loop of appropriate size, which you pass covertly around your hand; and your MAGICKAL WAND, placed twixt loop and flesh, can be induced to perform all manner of Bizarre Antics, the which you can devise in front of your mirror. The hair is invisible from any distance, even a very short one; and as you tap the wand reprovingly at trick's end, you break the loop, which falls unnoticed to the floor.

THE COIN *in the* EGG

 make no apologies for the fact that the last pair of tricks in this dissertation require somewhat more by way of preparation and skill than the others. There comes a time in the career of any CONJURER, no matter how humble his ambition, when he must attempt tricks that are a little more demanding than the common run.

The effect of the COIN IN THE EGG TRICK is this:– You request from the company the loan of a florin or a shilling, and ask that it be marked with a scratch or in some other wise. You explain that you intend to use this florin (or shilling) to make a coin omelette, for which you will also need a RAW EGG: such an egg you have conveniently to hand, all ready in its cup; and you pass the egg around while you expatiate on the delicious coin omelettes you have eaten during your sojourns in the Antipodes, &c., the Coin itself all the while visible in your hand. The egg returned, it is replaced in its cup, as with your free hand you dawdle with the coin; egg and cup together are passed to someone in the foremost row to look after carefully while you, as a preliminary, perform some other tricks with the coin. This you start to do, but then – oh! consternation! – somewhere you have erred, for the coin is lost! You beg forgiveness of its owner; then say that as a forfeit you will eat the raw egg. You seize it from its warden, and dash open the top with a spoon; then you suddenly look dubious; then suddenly (again) relieved; snatching up a pair of tweezers from your table you probe down delicately through the runny egg and withdraw – THE ORIGINAL COIN! Give a handkerchief to a member of the audience; place the dripping coin thereon; and have him dry it off, so that all can see it is indeed the coin that was marked, miraculously reappeared within the egg!

What you have done is this: Beforehand you have had the gardener (or his boy) cut a groove at the bottom of the inside of a wooden egg-cup; this groove to be correctly sized to hold a florin (or shilling) vertically. On receipt of the loaned coin, you have used palming to exchange it (as with "The 10/- Trick") for another which you already had with you. Before or during your "patter" about the joys of coin omelettes (choose the time that best suits you), you have secretly slipped the loaned coin into the groove within the egg-cup, all the while making a great play with the counterfeit. When the egg was returned from its inspection, you forced it down into the egg-cup, so that the coin penetrated the shell. Losing your sham coin was a pifflingly easy matter; and all the rest is plain . . .

THE CONFETTI EGG TRICK
~

Here is an illusion from the Nippon Isles. The effect is quite staggering; the Trick should not be performed in front of those of a highly-strung disposition. You take an egg, hold it high in the air above your head, and **crush it** (*the egg*); but instead of a deluge of sticky contents, what descends is a gentle shower of CONFETTI, which you brush casually from your shoulders before bowing to the inevitable accolade.

The egg, as the more discerning among you may have guessed, is not in its pristine condition at the start of the trick; rather, it has been toyed with aforehand. With a sharp needle, make two punctures, one at each end of a fresh egg expropriated from the kitchen. Re-calling your schoolboy days when you were accustomed to "*blowing*" stolen nest-eggs, in order to remove their

contents, do exactly the same now. The egg empty and well dried out, very carefully cut a small hole in its side, about the size of your finger-tip. Through the hole you may fill the empty shell with tiny pieces of torn-up coloured paper; commercially prepared confetti may be bought if you are in an EXTRAVAGANT HUMOUR. The egg refilled in this manner, conscientiously seal the hole by pasting over it a small piece of paper of coloration as close as possible to that of the shell itself.

Now all is done, and all you must needs accomplish for the presentation is exactly as described above; however, as you tighten your hand to crush the egg-shell, ensure that you grind it fairly forcefully (but as UN-OSTENTATIOUSLY as is feasible) with your thumb, such that the shreds of confetti rain down.

FINIS